Winter Dreams

English and Spanish

Written and Illustrated by Gabriella Eva Nagy

Copyright © 2016 Gabriella Eva Nagy
All rights reserved.

No part of this book may be reproduced in any manner without the written consent of the publisher except for brief excerpts in critical reviews or articles.

ISBN: 978-1-61244-525-0
Printed in the United States of America

Published by Halo Publishing International
1100 NW Loop 410
Suite 700 - 176
San Antonio, Texas 78213
Toll Free 1-877-705-9647
Website: www.halopublishing.com
E-mail: contact@halopublishing.com

My deep and sincere gratitude for God, for the inspiration and the dream to come true, and all my family and friends for their love, support, and encouragements.

Thousands of dancing snowflakes are falling gently,

Millones de copos de nieve bailando caen suavemente,

covering the land like a soft snow blanket.
Deer are leaping gracefully,

cubriendo la tierra en un suave manto de nieve.
Los venados saltan con gracia,

wild horses are galloping cheerfully,

caballos salvajes galopan alegremente,

red foxes are running swiftly,
embracing joyously the snowy dream world.

*zorros rojos corren rápidamente,
abrazando alegremente el mundo de ensueño nevado.*

The sound of woodpeckers knocking and colorful songbirds' cheerful twittering echoes through the frosted trees.

El sonido de los pájaros carpinteros golpeando y el colorido canto de los pájaros están twitteando ecos a través de los helados árboles.

Lively squirrels are chasing each other,
hedgehogs are snuggling under the crispy snow.

*Las ardillas animadas se persiguen una a otra,
erizos se acurrucan bajo la nieve crujiente.*

Bald eagles are circling in the midst of fluffy clouds,

*Las águilas calvas vuelan en círculos
en medio de nubes esponjosas,*

sleepy bear cubs are seeking a place to rest,

osos cachorros soñolientos buscan un lugar donde descansar,

lambs and swift-winged kingfishers
are admiring the glittering snow crystals.

*corderos y martines pescadores de alas rápidas
están admirando los brillantes cristales de nieve.*

The splendid cluster of sparkling stars are shining on
the still life of winter wonderland,
sweetly mesmerizing its lovely inhabitants.

*Un espléndido grupo de estrellas brillan en
la naturaleza del país de las maravillas del invierno
dulcemente hipnotizando a sus encantadores habitantes.*

www.ingramcontent.com/pod-product-compliance
Lightning Source LLC
Chambersburg PA
CBHW040007080526
44586CB00027B/2917